EZ Speed-Write™

EZ Speed-Write™

The Easy to Learn, User-Friendly, Speed-Writing System

EZ Learning Systems

EZ Speed-Write™

©2021 EZ Learning Systems

EZ Speed-Write™ is a trademark of EZ Learning Systems

EZ Learning Systems, New York

www.ezlearningsystems.com

Table of Contents

Introduction to EZ Speed-Write™

The EZ Speed-Write speed-writing system is an improved speed-writing method for note-taking purposes. It comprises three distinct elements: A core collection of strategically devised abbreviations; a qualified omission or substitution of letters in any given word; and a fundamental set of prefixes and suffixes. It is the unique combination and application of these elements that distinguishes EZ Speed-Write from other approaches to speed-writing. EZ Speed-Write sets a new standard for speed-writing methods.

The EZ Speed-Write system utilizes letters and common symbols. It is well suited for note-taking situations in which verbatim (i.e., word for word) transcription is not necessary.

Over the years, a number of such speed-writing methods have been developed. Many of the earlier methods were quite complicated and took several months, or longer, to learn. Those earlier methods have virtually completely fallen out of use.

The more recently developed of such methods are less complicated than the earlier ones, and do take less time to learn, but they, too, have their weaknesses. The main one being that the writing produced by them can be quite difficult to read (i.e., decipher), especially after some time has passed; making them less than practical, in the end.

The EZ Speed-Write system incorporates some practical and effective ideas found in other speed-writing methods, but it avoids elements which, though seemingly useful, can ultimately be problematic; especially those which can increase writing speed, but only at the expense of readability.

The EZ Speed-Write system was designed specifically to achieve a balance between writing speed and reading ease. It utilizes a manageable number of practical and effective speed-writing devices, and produces writing that is relatively easy to read; making it easy to learn, and user-friendly.

Incidentally, it should be noted that, although EZ Speed-Write is a speed-writing method, this does not imply that you should attempt to write any faster than usual when using it; and doing so may cause your writing to become illegible: The speed to be gained will come, instead, from the devices used.

One significant ancillary benefit of EZ Speed-Write is that it can be learned quickly. This is important because the easier and faster it is for you to learn a speed-writing method, the more likely you are to actually use it, and benefit from it.

Another such benefit is that it is a modular system. Starting with the first module, you can learn all the abbreviations and stop there if you wish; still deriving a benefit, with minimal effort. Or, you can continue and learn the next module, and the final module, as well; increasing your note-taking speed with each additional module.

Using the complete EZ Speed-Write system will enable you to increase your note-taking speed by as much as half, or more. To be sure, this is not as fast as some other methods have claimed for themselves; but clearly, given the importance of readability, what would be the point of taking fast notes, if you can't easily read and understand them afterwards? While other methods appear to overlook the issue of readability, focusing instead on writing speed, the EZ Speed-Write system realistically addresses both aspects of effective note-taking. In the end, what matters most is usability.

Whether you plan to use EZ Speed-Write for school, or work, or anything else, the ability to take fast, effective notes is a skill that will serve you well for years to come.

Note: The EZ Speed-Write system works with a computer keyboard, as well as with handwriting. The overall relative benefit, however, is greater with handwriting because of the difference between the time saved by omitting a written letter, and omitting a keystroke.

Congratulations on your decision to learn EZ Speed-Write!

EZ Speed-Write™ Module 1

Principle: Use a core collection of instantly recognizable abbreviations for high frequency words, and other common words and phrases.

In the EZ Speed-Write system, abbreviations are an essential, effective device that will account for a sizeable portion of everything you write. You will be using abbreviations for many of the most frequently used words and contractions in the English language, and for other common words and phrases, as well. Once learned, they will make sense to you and will instantly be recognizable. Using them extensively and consistently is a very easy way to increase your writing speed.

The principal criterion for using any abbreviation is that it must instantly be recognizable to you after you have written it. The other elements of the EZ Speed-Write system are not necessarily being applied to abbreviations. They won't need to be because abbreviations meeting the above criterion will always be effective in their own right.

Abbreviations for High Frequency Words

Below is a list of over 100 effective EZ Speed-Write abbreviations for many of the most frequently used words and contractions in the English language.

The list may seem large at first, but you should find most of the abbreviations to be quite intuitive, i.e., very easily learned and remembered. Each of them is based on a particular characteristic of the word being abbreviated. Once you see the relationship between an abbreviation and the word it represents, remembering and using it will be easy. As for any abbreviations you find less intuitive, with some additional thought they will be just as easy to learn.

Note: Some of the EZ Speed-Write abbreviations incorporate elements from the next module. For instance, the apostrophe (') is used to indicate (among other things) the word, "not"; and the en dash (–) is used, generally, to represent the sound of "th." This will become clear as you proceed.

High Frequency Word	EZ Speed-Write Abbreviation
able	abl
about	abt
after	aft
again	agn
another	an—
any	ny
anything	ny—
all	al
also	als
are	r
aren't	r'
be	b
been	bn
because	bec or bc
before	bef or bf
below	blw

High Frequency Word	EZ Speed-Write Abbreviation
between	btw
but	bt
can	cn
can't	cn'
cause	cz
could	cd
couldn't	cd'
did, do	d
didn't, don't	d'
done	dn
easy	ez
each	ea
effect, effective	eff
else	els
even	evn
ever	ev

High Frequency Word	EZ Speed-Write Abbreviation
every	evy
everything	evy–
except	exc
expect	exp
find, found	fnd
for	fr
from	fm
gave, give	gv
get, got	gt
good	gd
had	hd
hadn't	hd'
has	hs
hasn't	hs'
have	hv
haven't	hv'

High Frequency Word	EZ Speed-Write Abbreviation
how	hw
however	hwv
if	f
in	n
into	nt
isn't	is'
just	js
knew, know	kn
less	ls
like, look	lk
made	md
make	mk
many	mny
me, my	m
meet	mt
more	mr

High Frequency Word	EZ Speed-Write Abbreviation
most	mo
much	mch
must	ms
mustn't	ms'
never	nev
new, now	nw
next	nx
no	n
not	'
nothing	n—
off	ff
only	onl
other	o—
otherwise	o—w
our, out	ou
over	ov

High Frequency Word	EZ Speed-Write Abbreviation
part, put	pt
please	pls
real, really	rl
said	sd
say	sa
see	se
should	shd
shouldn't	shd'
some	sm
something	sm—
sure	sr
take, talk	tk
thank, think	—nk
that	—t
the	—
their, there	—r

High Frequency Word	EZ Speed-Write Abbreviation
them	–m
then, than	–n
they	–y
thing	–g
this, these	–s
to, too	t
time	tm
under	un
use	us or uz
used	usd
very	vy
want, went	wnt
was	ws
wasn't	ws'
were	wr
weren't	wr'

High Frequency Word	EZ Speed-Write Abbreviation
what	wht
when	whn
where	whr
which	whc
while	whi
who	wh
why	y
will, well	wl
with	w—
within	w—n
without	w—o
would	wd
wouldn't	wd'
yes	ys or y
you	u
your, you're	ur

Note: When using cursive (script) to write any of the above EZ Speed-Write abbreviations (or any EZ Speed-Write words, for that matter) that have an apostrophe between two letters, you may find it preferable not to disconnect the letters: You can insert the apostrophe after writing all the letters of the abbreviation.

Likewise, when writing the en dash, you may find it preferable not to disconnect cursive letters from it. If so, you can incorporate the en dash (or more precisely, an approximation of one) by simply elongating the connecting stroke to or from the letters.

Also note: Some of the EZ Speed-Write abbreviations are not abbreviations, per se. Rather, they are written as they would be, using the applicable elements of the EZ Speed-Write system. They are included here because the words are high frequency words.

Review of EZ Speed-Write Abbreviations for High Frequency Words:

For each word in the left-hand column, write the EZ Speed-Write abbreviation in the right-hand column. Then, cover up the left-hand column and recite the words by looking at and deciphering your EZ Speed-Write abbreviations.

High Frequency Word	EZ Speed-Write Abbreviation
able	
about	
after	
again	
another	
any	
anything	
all	
also	
are	
aren't	
be	
been	
because	
before	
below	

High Frequency Word	EZ Speed-Write Abbreviation
between	
but	
can	
can't	
cause	
could	
couldn't	
did, do	
didn't, don't	
done	
easy	
each	
effect, effective	
else	
even	
ever	

High Frequency Word	EZ Speed-Write Abbreviation
every	
everything	
except	
expect	
find, found	
for	
from	
gave, give	
get, got	
good	
had	
hadn't	
has	
hasn't	
have	
haven't	

High Frequency Word	EZ Speed-Write Abbreviation
how	
however	
if	
in	
into	
isn't	
just	
knew, know	
less	
like, look	
made	
make	
many	
me, my	
meet	
more	

High Frequency Word	EZ Speed-Write Abbreviation
most	
much	
must	
mustn't	
never	
new, now	
next	
no	
not	
nothing	
off	
only	
other	
otherwise	
our, out	
over	

High Frequency Word	EZ Speed-Write Abbreviation
part, put	
please	
real, really	
said	
say	
see	
should	
shouldn't	
some	
something	
sure	
take, talk	
thank, think	
that	
the	
their, there	

High Frequency Word	EZ Speed-Write Abbreviation
them	
then, than	
they	
thing	
this, these	
to, too	
time	
under	
use	
used	
very	
want, went	
was	
wasn't	
were	
weren't	

High Frequency Word	EZ Speed-Write Abbreviation
what	
when	
where	
which	
while	
who	
why	
will, well	
with	
within	
without	
would	
wouldn't	
yes	
you	
your, you're	

Things to do now...

Practice using these EZ Speed-Write abbreviations simply by writing each of them a few times and making up some short phrases that include the ones you find most intuitive. Then, do the same with more abbreviations from the list after you have mastered the prior ones, saving the ones that you may find less intuitive until the end. Continue doing this until you have learned them all.

You should also practice by recording yourself saying the words, and then writing the EZ Speed-Write abbreviations while listening to the recording. Practice deciphering what you write, as well. You will want to become fluent both in writing what you see and hear, and in reading what you write.

As stated earlier, it won't take you much time to learn these EZ Speed-Write abbreviations because most of them are quite intuitive.

Abbreviations for Other Common Words

In addition to using abbreviations for high frequency words, you should use them for other common words. Below is a list of some effective abbreviations for other common words. Some of them are not exclusive to EZ Speed-Write.

Common Word	EZ Speed-Write Abbreviation
accept	accp
account	acct
additional	addl
amount	amt
appointment	appt
approximate	appx
assistant	asst
attachment	attch
attention	attn
average	avg
building	bldg
department	dept
information	info
management	mgmt
market	mkt
maximum	max

Common Word	EZ Speed-Write Abbreviation
meeting	mtg
minimum	min
nevertheless	nvtls
original	orig
people	ppl
question	q
require	req
required	reqd
requirement	reqt
responsibility	respy
responsible	respl
sometimes	stms
today	tda
tomorrow	tmw
week	wk
year	yr

This list is not exhaustive. The purpose of the list is to give you some examples and ideas for developing or adopting other abbreviations for other common words, as well.

Some EZ Speed-Write abbreviations may be combined, or, as you will see later on, incorporated into other words, in order to take advantage of the abbreviation. It may be helpful to add a hyphen (-) before, after, or between the EZ Speed-Write abbreviation(s), as appropriate. In some cases, the hyphen won't be needed to make the intended word clear, but in others, it will definitely be helpful, or necessary.

Review of EZ Speed-Write Abbreviations for Other Common Words:

For each word in the left-hand column, write the EZ Speed-Write abbreviation in the right-hand column. Then, cover up the left-hand column and recite the words by looking at and deciphering your EZ Speed-Write abbreviations.

Common Word	EZ Speed-Write Abbreviation
accept	
account	
additional	
amount	
appointment	
approximate	
assistant	
attachment	
attention	
average	
building	
department	
information	
management	
market	
maximum	

Common Word	EZ Speed-Write Abbreviation
meeting	
minimum	
nevertheless	
original	
people	
question	
require	
required	
requirement	
responsibility	
responsible	
sometimes	
today	
tomorrow	
week	
year	

Things to do now...

Practice using the EZ Speed-Write abbreviations for these common words in the same way you practiced the EZ Speed-Write abbreviations for high frequency words.

In addition to the words on this list, you should develop or adopt abbreviations for words that are common for your own writing circumstances, e.g., specific courses, work, community organizations, etc.

Abbreviations for Common Phrases

You will also benefit by using abbreviations for common phrases. Below are some effective abbreviations for common phrases. Again, some of them are not exclusive to EZ Speed-Write.

Common Phrase	EZ Speed-Write Abbreviation
all things considered	atc
as long as	ala
any and all	aal
as far as we know	afawk
as soon as possible	asap
by the way	btw
compare and contrast	cac
estimated time of arrival	eta
everything else being equal	eebe
for all intents and purposes	faiap
for the sake of argument	ftsa
for your information	fyi
in any event	iae
it's a matter of opinion	iamo
more (most) important	mi!
need to know	ntk

Common Phrase	EZ Speed-Write Abbreviation
thank you	ty
to be continued	tbc
to be determined	tbd
we don't know	wdk
with respect to	wrt

Again, this list is not exhaustive. The purpose of the list is to give you some examples and ideas for developing or adopting other abbreviations for other common phrases, as well.

Review of EZ Speed-Write Abbreviations for Common Phrases:

For each phrase in the left-hand column, write the EZ Speed-Write abbreviation in the right-hand column. Then, cover up the left-hand column and recite the phrases by looking at and deciphering your EZ Speed-Write abbreviations.

Common Phrase	EZ Speed-Write Abbreviation
all things considered	
as long as	
any and all	
as far as we know	
as soon as possible	
by the way	
compare and contrast	
estimated time of arrival	
everything else being equal	
for all intents and purposes	
for the sake of argument	
for your information	
in any event	
it's a matter of opinion	
more (most) important	
need to know	

Common Phrase	EZ Speed-Write Abbreviation
thank you	
to be continued	
to be determined	
we don't know	
with respect to	

Things to do now…

Practice using the EZ Speed-Write abbreviations for common phrases in the same way you practiced the other EZ Speed-Write abbreviations.

In addition to the phrases on this list, you should develop or adopt abbreviations for phrases that are common for your own writing circumstances, e.g., specific courses, work, community organizations, etc.

Symbol Abbreviations

In addition to using letter-based abbreviations, you should use a number of symbols as abbreviations for common words and phrases. Some examples of commonly used, effective symbol abbreviations follow below.

Note: Some of the symbols are not available as a simple keystroke on a computer keyboard. For those symbols, you may choose suitable substitutes, or simply forego their use.

Word/Phrase	Symbol
and	+ or &
and so on, etc.	…
approximately	≈
at	@
change	Δ
decrease, less	↓
equal, same	=
increase, more	↑ or ^
important, priority	!
leads to, causes	→ or >
less than	<
money, cost	$
more or less	+/-
more than	>
number	#
question	?
therefore	∴

These are the most commonly used, effective symbol abbreviations. Again, this list is not exhaustive. The purpose of the list is to give you some examples and ideas for choosing other symbol abbreviations, as well.

Review of Symbol Abbreviations:

For each word or phrase in the left-hand column write the symbol in the right-hand column. Then, cover up the left-hand column and recite the words or phrases, looking at the symbols.

Word/Phrase	Symbol
and	
and so on, etc.	
approximately	
at	
change	
decrease, less	
equal, same	
increase, more	
important, priority	
leads to, causes	
less than	
money, cost	
more or less	
more than	
number	
question	
therefore	

Things to do now...

Practice using the symbol abbreviations for common words and phrases in the same way you practiced the other EZ Speed-Write abbreviations.

Final thoughts on EZ Speed-Write Module 1:

If you went no further with the EZ Speed-Write system than using the abbreviations in module 1, you would still have the ability to take faster notes, with minimal effort. For some, this will be enough of a benefit. Additionally, your notes will be very easy to read, since you are not altering the appearance of any substantive content.

EZ Speed-Write Module 1 provides a very simple and effective component of the EZ Speed-Write system. You may wish to use only module 1 for a while, before proceeding to the next module.

EZ Speed-Write™ Module 2

Principle(s): Write enough of the letters of a word as necessary to maintain its recognizability; use an indicator to represent or modify the sounds of certain letters; and when helpful, use the limited group of phonetic substitutes to indicate the sounds of certain letter combinations.

All speed-writing methods are based on the idea that, generally, for any given word, one or more letters may be omitted in order to save time writing, while still maintaining its recognizability (either by itself, or in context).

This module provides a variety of approaches to omitting letters in any given word. It comprises a number of effective speed-writing devices; some of which have already been introduced in module 1. They will be discussed separately, in the order stated above.

The devices are not meant to be mechanically or rigidly applied. They allow for some flexibility based on personal preferences. In a short time, you will develop the ability to intuitively apply the devices, as appropriate, as you are writing.

The first element of the module involves the fundamental idea of writing enough of the letters of a word as necessary to maintain its recognizability. This will vary from word to word. There are three approaches to accomplishing this: 1) Omitting short vowels, generally, other than those at the beginning or end of the word (or immediately following a prefix), 2) omitting silent letters, generally, and 3) truncating (shortening) familiar or otherwise recognizable words.

A short vowel essentially is a vowel that sounds different than the name of the letter, itself. A vowel used in a way such that it has a long vowel sound other than that of the letter itself, e.g., "ski," should generally be treated as a long vowel. (Long vowels should almost always be retained.)

A silent letter is a letter that is not heard in any given word, e.g., the "g" and the "h," in "right," or a letter whose sound is adequately represented by another letter in the word, e.g., the "c," in "luck," or one "p," in "supply."

Truncating is accomplished, generally, by omitting the last few or more letters of a word, or by doing so, but retaining the last letter, and when helpful, preceding it with an apostrophe. It may be used for any word that would retain its recognizability after being truncated. In general, truncating tends to work better with longer words.

The approach(es) that should be utilized for any given word will depend, in part, on the word itself. For some words, one approach may be preferable to another; while for other words, more than one approach may be used effectively. The following examples will demonstrate this. Context will usually also be a factor. With practice, you will soon be able to intuitively choose which approach(es) to utilize in any given situation.

Now, let's look at our first example:

Word	EZ Speed-Write
friend	frnd

In this example, we are omitting the silent "i," and the short "e." Here, the short vowel may safely be omitted, as the actual word remains recognizable without it.

It is quite frequently helpful, nevertheless, to retain a short vowel in an accented syllable, or in the initial syllable of a word.

It should be pointed out that for some short words, such as those which contain only one (long) vowel, it might be the case that no letters would be omitted, e.g., "mind." This actually has a beneficial effect because it will contribute to an overall visual framework that enhances the readability of your notes.

Let's consider our next example:

Word	EZ Speed-Write
apple	apl

In this example we are omitting a silent (double) "p," and the silent "e." For some words, leaving a double consonant or a consonant combination (even one that involves silent consonants) intact can help you in recognizing them, based on the visual characteristics of the letter combinations involved. In this case, one double consonant may safely be omitted.

Let's continue with another example:

Word	EZ Speed-Write
redevelopment	redvelpm

Here, we are omitting the first short "e" and the short "o," as well as all the letters after the "m." The short, third "e" is being retained to demonstrate how retaining a short vowel in an accented syllable of a word can sometimes be helpful for readability (especially after some time has passed). Most other speed-writing methods call for the automatic omission of all of such vowels, which can sometimes cause confusion. This example also demonstrates the use of truncating where a certain suffix is being implied by one of its letters, making the intended word clear.

As a final observation about using the above devices, keep in mind that some words may be more easily discernable than others because of the way the remaining consonants will appear. This is why you will want to consider using the options discussed above, e.g., retaining certain short vowels, or certain consonant combinations.

Let's look at a few final examples for this section:

Word	EZ Speed-Write
demolish	demol
demolition	demol'n
demonstration	demo

These examples demonstrate that sometimes we can truncate a word by, 1) omitting the last few or more letters of a word because the intended word is familiar or otherwise recognizable, and clearly is being implied by the first few or more letters; or 2) omitting all but the final letter of such letters and when helpful, adding an apostrophe, indicating the omission of a group of letters before the final letter, or 3) omitting all such letters where the word is commonly truncated in a certain way.

Truncating should be used regularly in your writing (generally, at least once per line or sentence), as truncated words create visual anchors that will enhance the readability of your notes.

The next element of this module involves the use of an en dash (–) (written about twice as long as a hyphen, and indicated on a computer keyboard by two consecutive hyphen keystrokes) to indicate the "th" sound; and the use of an apostrophe after the letters "c," "g," "s," "t," and "x," to indicate the range of sounds of "ch," "j," "sh," and "zh"; and to indicate the sounds of vowels that create two syllables.

Let's look at a few examples using the en dash to represent the "th" sound:

Word	EZ Speed-Write
breathe	bre–
thirst	–rst
weather	w–r

Now, let's look at a few examples using the apostrophe to alter the sound of various consonants:

Word	EZ Speed-Write
conscience	conc'nc
charge	chrg'
station	stat'n

Most commonly, when the apostrophe is used in this way, the actual sounds involved are, "zhun" or "shun" (sion, tion), "shul" (cial, tial), "shus" (cious, xious), and "shents" (cience, tients). You will see this device again in the next module, in the context of EZ Speed-Write suffixes.

In some speed-writing methods no device is used to indicate an intended alteration of sound. We have found the use of the apostrophe to be helpful for such a purpose (in addition to its other uses).

Now, let's look at a few examples using the apostrophe to represent the sounds of vowels that create two syllables:

Word	EZ Speed-Write
delineate	dlin't
evaluate	eval't
meander	m'ndr

Though the apostrophe is used in more than one way in the EZ Speed-Write system, it will almost never be unclear how it is being used in any given instance.

Note: In EZ Speed-Write, the apostrophe is not used in accordance with ordinary English usage. Rather, it is simply omitted in such circumstances. Context will make it clear when one is to be inferred.

The last element of this module involves the use of a limited group of phonetic substitutes to indicate the sounds of certain letter combinations.

In the EZ Speed-Write system, phonetic substitutes may be used to represent certain letter combinations that create a single sound. Unlike other speed-writing methods, the EZ Speed-Write system generally does not use phonetic substitutes to replace single letters.

We have found that other speed-writing methods tend to over-use phonetic substitutes. We believe, for example, that it is more difficult to recognize "jsntrk," as the word, "geocentric," than it is to recognize "g'cntrc." The use of too many phonetic substitutes tends to cause visual confusion by making the words look unfamiliar, i.e., too different from the actual words, which can interfere with deciphering.

There are no phonetic substitutes in the EZ Speed-Write system for vowel combinations that are sounded as two syllables: This is addressed in the previous section.

Below is the limited group of phonetic substitutes in the EZ Speed-Write system.

Common Sound Combination	EZ Speed-Write Phonetic Substitute
eau (e.g., "bureau," "chateau")	o
ei, et, ey (e.g., "weigh," "ballet," "convey")	a
ew, oe, oo (e.g., "pew," "shoe," "woo")	u
oi, oy (e.g., "point," "toy")	y
ua, ui, au, ou (i.e., generally, the "w" sound)	w*

*The use of this phonetic substitute is not necessary for any word in which its sound follows the letter "q."

This list of EZ Speed-Write phonetic substitutes addresses the most common sound combinations that lend themselves well to phonetic substitutes. Though there are many more sound combinations in the English language, the above group of phonetic substitutes addresses a sufficient number of them and effectively approximates their sound variations.

You may be inclined, at times, not to use phonetic substitutes. Consider, for instance, the word, "sought," which may be written as, "swt," using the applicable phonetic substitute. You may find it preferable to write it without the phonetic substitute, as, "sot," or perhaps, "sght" (see the earlier comment in this module regarding silent consonant combinations) because by writing it in either of those other ways it would more closely resemble the intended word.

Things to do now...

Now, it's time for some practice. Look at each of the words in the column below and write the word utilizing the devices in module 2 next to it. Then, cover up the word column and recite the words by looking at and deciphering your EZ Speed-Write words.

Word	EZ Speed-Write
accomplish	
affluent	
aloud, allowed	
altogether	
beau	
beam	
booted	
bouquet	
canoe	
champagne	
concerned	
colloquial	
conscience	
cachet	
damage	

Word	EZ Speed-Write
diameter	
eulogize	
evaluate	
faux	
feather	
gauge	
heightened	
issue	
loose	
manage	
passage	
patience	
plateau	
plough, plow	
power	

Word	EZ Speed-Write
prey	
quick	
quiet	
quite	
reality	
reign	
relinquish	
review	
school	
shoe	
special	
tourist	
theatrical	
virtuous	
weigh	

Word	EZ Speed-Write Solution
accomplish	acmplsh
affluent	afl'nt
aloud, allowed	alwd
altogether	altg–r
beau	bo
beam	bem
booted	butd
bouquet	boqa or buqa
canoe	cnu
champagne	chmpan
concerned	cncernd
colloquial	cloq'l
conscience	conc'nc
cachet	cacha
damage	damg'

Word	EZ Speed-Write Solution
diameter	d'mtr
eulogize	ulg'iz
evaluate	eval't
faux	fo
feather	f–r
gauge	gag'
heightened	hitnd
issue	is'u
loose	lus
manage	mang'
passage	pasg'
patience	pat'nc
plateau	plto
plough, plow	plw
power	pwr

Word	EZ Speed-Write Solution
prey	pra
quick	qk
quiet	q't
quite	qit
reality	r'lty
reign	ran
relinquish	rlnqsh
review	rvu
school	scul
shoe	shu
special	spec'l
tourist	turst
theatrical	—'trcl
virtuous	vrt's
weigh	wa

Final thoughts on EZ Speed-Write Modules 1 and 2:

If you went no further with the EZ Speed-Write system than using EZ Speed-Write Modules 1 and 2, you would still have the ability to take notes noticeably faster.

You may wish to use only modules 1 and 2 for a while, before proceeding to the final module.

EZ Speed-Write™ Module 3

Principle: Use the fundamental set of EZ Speed-Write prefixes and suffixes.

Prefixes and suffixes are letters added to the beginning or the end of a word root, respectively, which change its meaning. For our purposes, the main issue is how they can best be represented.

Prefixes and suffixes are used frequently enough to warrant using abbreviated forms for a sufficient number of them in any comprehensive speed-writing method. The ones utilized here have been selected primarily based on frequency of use. Any prefixes or suffixes for which EZ Speed-Write does not have an abbreviated form may be spelled out, or written utilizing other applicable EZ Speed-Write elements.

There may be instances where you are not sure whether a word actually contains a prefix or a suffix, as such. Generally, it won't matter because the intended word, as written in EZ Speed-Write, would usually be clear whether you treated it as having one, or not.

EZ Speed-Write prefixes and suffixes may sometimes be used as word beginnings or word endings, for words that do not contain prefixes or suffixes, as such. Whether you choose to do so will depend, in some cases, on the resulting appearance/readability of a given word, by itself, or in context, and in other cases, on personal preference.

The forward slash used in certain EZ Speed-Write prefixes (i.e., most of the ones for which the actual prefix comprises two syllables) is a helpful device in the EZ Speed-Write system because it signals the presence of a prefix where it might not otherwise be obvious. When you see it in your notes, you will know one is present, and you will know not to simply sound out the letters.

The apostrophe used in certain EZ Speed-Write prefixes and suffixes is another helpful device in the EZ Speed-Write system. When you see it in this context in your notes, it will signal the presence of a prefix or suffix and, again, you will know not to simply sound out the letters.

Note: When a prefix or a suffix is, or includes the accented syllable of a word, you may sometimes wish to retain a vowel contained therein, as doing so can assist you in recognizing the intended word. You will see this applied in some of the solutions in this module. Additionally, be sure to retain a short vowel that follows a prefix, as it will almost always make the intended word more easily recognizable.

In some cases, a prefix or suffix may need to be spelled out because the intended word may otherwise be ambiguous, despite the context. This is especially true in cases where the ambiguity may be significant or problematic. For example, the EZ Speed-Write prefix for "pre" and "pro" is, "pr." The words, "prescribe" and "proscribe" mean two very different things, but would be written in the same way if you did not specify the prefix. Unless context would eliminate the ambiguity, the appropriate prefix should be spelled out.

Prefixes

Below is the fundamental set of prefixes with their EZ Speed-Write equivalents. You may notice that some of them have appeared in module 2, but there, they were the result of the application of devices in that module; here, they are formalized as EZ Speed-Write prefixes. There is no need to try to remember all of them at once. You can practice them in groups, incorporating them into your writing gradually.

Prefix	EZ Speed-Write Prefix
ante, anti, auto	at/
be, bi	b
bio	b'
circum	cr/
com	cm
con	cn
contra/o, counter	ct/
de, di	d
des, dis, dys	ds
dia	d'
e/inter, e/intra, e/intro	nt/
equa, equi	eq
ex, ax	x
exter, extra, extro	xt/
for, fore	fr
hyper	hy/
hypo	ho/

Prefix	EZ Speed-Write Prefix
macro	ma/
mal	ml
m(vowel)n	mn
m(vowel)s	ms
mega	mg/
micro	mi/
mid	md
multi	mt/
non	'
omni	om/
over	ov/
p(vowel)r, pr(vowel)	pr
para, pari, peri, piro	pr/
post	po'
pseudo	ps/
re	r
rctro	rt/

Prefix	EZ Speed-Write Prefix
semi	sm/
sub	sb
sup	sp
super, supra	su/
sur	sr
tel, tele	tl
trans	t'
ulti, ultra	ul/
under	un/

Things to do now…

Now, it's time for some practice with the prefixes. Look at each of the words in the column below, and write the word incorporating the EZ Speed-Write prefixes next to it (you may also incorporate the devices from module 2, as demonstrated in the solutions). Then, cover up the word column and recite the words by looking at and deciphering your EZ Speed-Write words.

Prefix Word	EZ Speed-Write
antibody	
autonomy	
benefit	
bilateral	
biometric	
circumference	
circumstance	
complete	
commute	
condition	
contrary	
converted	
disagree	
dispense	
divert	
equip	

Prefix Word	EZ Speed-Write
exclude	
external	
extradite	
foresee	
formal	
hyperactive	
hypothesis	
internal	
introduce	
malign	
malleable	
manage	
mandate	
manual	
megaplex	
mental	

Prefix Word	EZ Speed-Write
mention	
microscope	
misapply	
mistake	
montage	
multifaceted	
multiple	
noncompliance	
omnibus	
overdraft	
parameter	
paradigm	
permeate	
personal	
posthaste	
precise	

Prefix Word	EZ Speed-Write
prescribe	
pseudonym	
reapply	
release	
retrospect	
semicircle	
subliminal	
supply	
televised	
transcribe	
ultimate	
understate	

Prefix Word	EZ Speed-Write Solution
antibody	at/bdy
autonomy	at/nmy
benefit	bnfit
bilateral	blatrl
biometric	b'metrc
circumference	cr/frnc
circumstance	cr/stnc
complete	cmplet
commute	cmut
condition	cndit'n
contrary	ct/ry
converted	cnvertd
disagree	dsagre
dispense	dspens
divert	dvert
equip	eqp

Prefix Word	EZ Speed-Write Solution
exclude	xclud
external	xt/nl
extradite	xt/dit
foresee	frse
formal	frml
hyperactive	hy/actv
hypothesis	ho/–sis
internal	nt/nl
introduce	nt/duc
malign	mlin
malleable	mal'bl
manage	mang'
mandate	mndat
manual	mn'l
megaplex	mg/plx
mental	mntl

Prefix Word	EZ Speed-Write Solution
mention	mnt'n
microscope	mi/scop
misapply	msaply
mistake	mstak
montage	mntg'
multifaceted	mt/facetd
multiple	mt/pl
noncompliance	'cmpl'nc
omnibus	om/bs
overdraft	ov/drft
parameter	pr/mtr
paradigm	pr/dim
permeate	prm't
personal	prsnl
posthaste	po'hast
precise	prcis

Prefix Word	EZ Speed-Write Solution
prescribe	pr(e)scrib
pseudonym	ps/nm
reapply	raply
release	rles
retrospect	rt/spct
semicircle	sm/cir
subliminal	sblmnl
supply	sply
televised	tlvisd
transcribe	t'crib
ultimate	ul/mt
understate	un/stat

Suffixes

Below is the fundamental set of suffixes with their EZ Speed-Write equivalents. Again, you may notice that some of them have appeared in module 2, where they resulted from the application of devices in that module; while here, they are formalized as EZ Speed-Write suffixes. There is no need to try to remember all of them at once. You can practice them in groups, incorporating them into your writing gradually.

Suffix	EZ Speed-Write Suffix
acy	cy
age, dge	g'
ality	'ty
(a/i)bility	b'ty
(a/i)ble	bl
cial	c'l
cious	c's
ed	d
en	n
er, ar, or	r
es, ies (as pl. for y ending), s	s
esque	sq
ful	fl
hood	h'
ian, ion	'n
ied	'd
ing	'g

Suffix	EZ Speed-Write Suffix
ious, ous	's
ise (as in, "wise"), ize	'z
ish	sh
ive	v
(vowel)l, le	l
less	ls
(o)logy	'gy
ment	m'
ness	ns
ship	shp
sion, sian	s'n
tial	t'l
tion	t'n
ure	'r
ward	w'
xious	x's
(a/al/e/i)ly, ley	ly

Suffix	EZ Speed-Write Suffix
ify	fy
(et/it)y	ty
y, ey	y

Note: When the use of a EZ Speed-Write suffix would otherwise result in two immediately adjacent apostrophes, omit one of them.

Also note: Sometimes a suffix, such as, "es" (plural), or "ed" (past tense) may be ignored because context may make the intended word clear without having to write the EZ Speed-Write suffix.

Things to do now...

Now, it's time for some practice with the suffixes. Look at each of the words in the column below, and write the word incorporating the EZ Speed-Write suffixes next to it (you may also incorporate the devices from module 2, as demonstrated in the solutions). Then, cover up the word column and recite the words by looking at and deciphering your EZ Speed-Write words.

Note: The EZ Speed-Write prefixes should also be incorporated into this exercise.

Suffix Word	EZ Speed-Write
accessible	
applicable	
biology	
bring	
bundle	
conceded	
contentment	
creative	
departure	
divisibility	
doubtful	
endure	
excitement	
forward	
friendship	
grateful	

Suffix Word	EZ Speed-Write
handle	
helpful	
hurdle	
interceding	
kindness	
little	
mending	
metal	
meter	
needless	
needlessly	
nourish	
obliquely	
opposed	
outside	
ownership	

Suffix Word	EZ Speed-Write
partial	
permissive	
powerful	
precision	
presidential	
profoundly	
provider	
receded	
recessed	
relative	
remained	
remedied	
requisitioned	
reward	
showing	
skillfully	

Suffix Word	EZ Speed-Write
spacious	
specially	
subtle	
superficial	
surmise	
telling	
thankful	
translation	
united	
validity	
verify	

Suffix Word	EZ Speed-Write Solution
accessible	accesbl
applicable	aplicbl
biology	b'gy
bring	br'g
bundle	bndl
conceded	cncedd
contentment	cntentm'
creative	cr'tv
departure	dprt'r
divisibility	dvsb'ty
doubtful	dwtfl
endure	end'r
excitement	xitm'
forward	frw'
friendship	frndshp
grateful	gratfl

Suffix Word	EZ Speed-Write Solution
handle	hndl
helpful	hlpfl
hurdle	hrdl
interceding	nt/ced'g
kindness	kindns
little	ltl
mending	mnd'g
metal	mtl
meter	metr
needless	nedls
needlessly	nedlsly
nourish	nursh
obliquely	obliqly
opposed	oposd
outside	ousid
ownership	onrshp

Suffix Word	EZ Speed-Write Solution
partial	prt'l
permissive	prmisv
powerful	pwrfl
precision	prcis'n
presidential	prsdent'l
profoundly	prfndly
provider	prvidr
receded	rcedd
recessed	rcesd
relative	rltv
remained	rmand
remedied	remd'd
requisitioned	rqsit'nd
reward	rw'
showing	sho'g
skillfully	skilfly

Suffix Word	EZ Speed-Write Solution
spacious	spac's
specially	spec'ly
subtle	sutl
superficial	su/fc'l
surmise	srm'z
telling	tl'g
thankful	—nkfl
translation	t'lat'n
united	unitd
validity	vlidty
verify	vrfy

Additional practice for EZ Speed-Write Modules 1, 2, and 3:

For each sentence below, write the EZ Speed-Write sentence beneath it, utilizing the speed-writing devices in all the modules.

That is really important, but it wasn't considered.

They will certainly have to make a better selection.

All those involved were communicating really well.

Those factors must always be evaluated together.

There are so many comparisons that could be made.

Help shouldn't have been necessary at that time.

It was more a question of opinion, as opposed to fact.

That didn't do much good, apparently.

The project was completed on time and under budget.

It isn't likely to matter much, given their preference.

Additional practice for EZ Speed-Write Modules 1, 2, and 3, continued:

It would be a good idea to stop and think about it.

We know they did well, as they were better prepared.

They would have preferred a different result.

That was an incredible turn of events.

A good understanding is a requirement for success.

That would have been a very good approach.

Now would be a perfect time to study this.

Solutions to additional practice for EZ Speed-Write Modules 1, 2, and 3:

—t is rl import, bt it ws' cnsidrd.

—y wl cert hv t mk a betr select'n.

Al —os involv wr cmuncat'g rl wl.

—os factrs ms alwa b eval'd tg—r.

—r r so mny compar —t cd b md.

Hlp shd' hv bn necc at —t tm.

It ws mr a ? of opin, as opp t fct.

—t d' d mch gd, appar.

— proj ws compl on tm & un budg.

It is' lkly t matr mch, gvn —r pref.

Solutions to additional practice for EZ Speed-Write Modules 1, 2, and 3, continued:

It wd b a gd idea t stp & –nk abt it.

W kn –y d wl, as –y wr betr prepd.

–y wd hv pref a diff rsult.

–t ws an incred trn of evnts.

A gd underst is a reqt fr succ.

–t wd hv bn a vy gd appro.

Nw wd b a perf tm t stdy –s.

Concluding remarks on the effect of speed-writing devices on word readability:

As you are developing your skills in the EZ Speed-Write system, you will also be developing an awareness of how the EZ Speed-Write words are beginning to appear on the page, as you are writing them. Occasionally, you may find that any given word might begin to take on a somewhat ambiguous appearance. In most cases, context will supply the necessary clarification. If you have any concerns, however, there is no need to rewrite the word; rather, simply omit fewer of the remaining letters, as you continue to write, thereby allowing the intended word to becomes sufficiently clear. You will generally find this to be a very easy and effective adjustment procedure to use, as appropriate.

Conclusion

That's the entire EZ Speed-Write speed-writing system! You now have at your fingertips, a very effective, easily learned, and user-friendly speed-writing system. All you need to do now is continue to practice.

Note: The English language is a fairly complex language with many nuances in spelling and pronunciation. Although the EZ Speed-Write system may easily be applied to 99% of the words you will write, you will always come across words for which a EZ Speed-Write system solution may be elusive. In some cases, you may wish to write such words out in their entirety. In other cases, you should be able to come close to an optimal EZ Speed-Write solution.

Also note: It is strongly recommended that you not use EZ Speed-Write, 1) for any terminology that is new or unfamiliar, 2) for stand-alone words with no clear context to aid in deciphering, 3) in note section headings (EZ Speed-Write abbreviations, however, may be used), or 4) for proper nouns, except for unmistakable ones, e.g., "Abrhm Lincn."

After completing the exercises in this book, practice applying the EZ Speed-Write system to television, radio, and print media, in the same way. That way, you will have an abundant supply of materials available for you to develop your skills.

As you apply the EZ Speed-Write system, be sure to use conventional real-time editing in your note-taking, as appropriate. For example, suppose you were going to take notes on the sentence – "It is agreed that the most important factors involved in this case would be size and weight." Using EZ Speed-Write, instead of writing, "It is agred –t – mo imprtnt factrs involv n –s cas wd b siz & wat," you would write something more like, "Agred: Mi! factrs – siz & wat." This, of course, will further increase your note-taking speed.

It is recommended that you review your notes as soon as possible after taking them so you can make any necessary clarifications or corrections while the material is still fresh in your mind. That will be the best time for you to do so.

Finally, although EZ Speed-Write is a system, it is flexible enough, as has been noted at various times herein, to be adaptable to individual preferences. Given the nuances of the English language, this is a definite advantage of EZ Speed-Write.

We wish you much success with your newfound skill.

Ty fr ur nt/st n lrn'g EZ Sped-rit!